P9-DUT-917

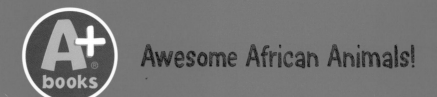

Chimpanzees Are Awesome!

By Megan Cooley Peterson

Consultant: Jackie Gai, DVM
Captive Wildlife Veterinarian

CAPSTONE PRESS
a capstone imprint

A+ Books are published by Capstone Press,
1710 Roe Crest Drive, North Mankato, Minnesota 56003
www.capstonepub.com

Library of Congress Cataloging-in-Publication Data
Peterson, Megan Cooley, author.
  Chimpanzees are awesome! / by Megan Cooley Peterson.
      pages cm. — (A+ books. Awesome African animals)
  Summary: "Describes the characteristics, habitat, behavior, life cycle, and threats to chimpanzees living in the wild of Africa"—Provided by publisher.
  Audience: Ages 5–8.
  Audience: K to grade 3.
  Includes bibliographical references and index.
  ISBN 978-1-4914-1759-1 (library binding)
  ISBN 978-1-4914-1765-2 (paperback)
  ISBN 978-1-4914-1771-3 (eBook PDF)
  1. Chimpanzees—Juvenile literature. 2. Animals—Africa—Juvenile literature. I. Title.

QL737.P94P48 2015
599.885—dc23   2014023668

Editorial Credits
Erika Shores and Mari Bolte, editors; Cynthia Della-Rovere, designer;
Svetlana Zhurkin, media researcher; Morgan Walters, production specialist

Photo Credits
Alamy: Ariadne Van Zandbergen, 13, Juergen Ritterbach, 16; Dreamstime: Jens Klingebiel, 10–11; iStockphotos: SeppFriedhuber, 4–5; Minden Pictures: Cyril Ruoso, 19, 20, 23–24, 28, Suzi Eszterhas, 21, 24–25; Newscom: imageBROKER/FLPA/Jurgen & Christine Sohns, 26, Mint Images/Frans Lanting, 14–15, Photoshot/NHPA/David Higgs, 9; Science Source: Michel Gunther, 17 (top); Shutterstock: Andrzej Grzegorczyk, 6, Black Sheep Media (grass), throughout, Eric Isselee, cover (bottom, top right), 1 (bottom), 22, 32, Ferenc Szelepcsenyi, 29, LeonP, cover (top left), 8, M. Unal Ozmen (banana), cover, 1, Pal Teravagimov (forest background), back cover and throughout, Quang Ho (banana leaf), throughout, Sam DCruz, 18, Sergey Uryadnikov, 7 (back), Stephen Meese, 7 (front), Svetlana Foote, 12, Worakit Sirijinda, 27

Note to Parents, Teachers, and Librarians
This Awesome African Animals book uses full color photographs and a nonfiction format to introduce the concept of chimpanzees. *Chimpanzees Are Awesome!* is designed to be read aloud to a pre-reader or to be read independently by an early reader. Photographs help listeners and early readers understand the text and concepts discussed. The book encourages further learning by including the following sections: Table of Contents, Glossary, Read More, Internet Sites, and Index. Early readers may need assistance using these features.

Printed in China by Nordica.
0914/CA21401520
092014   008470NORDS15

Table of Contents

Chatty Chimpanzees

A chimpanzee swings from branch to branch. It climbs down and hugs a friend. Then the chimps dig through each other's fur. They pick out bugs and dirt.

Touch is an important way chimpanzees communicate. They groom and kiss each other. They hug and tickle.

Chimpanzees "talk" to each other in many ways. These primates scream, bark, yell, and laugh. They chase each other and make faces. Chimpanzees don't hide their feelings. They are social animals that need to spend time with other chimps.

6

A Chimpanzee's Body

Chimpanzees belong to
the ape family. Gorillas,
orangutans, and humans
are also apes.

Adult chimpanzees stand up to 5.5 feet (1.7 meters) tall. They weigh up to 150 pounds (68 kilograms.) Male chimps are larger than females.

A chimpanzee's face looks a lot like a human's. Chimps have small noses and eyes that face forward. Like us, they can see in color. Sight is their most important sense.

Brown or black hair covers a chimpanzee's body. Like humans, their hair grays as they age. A chimp may puff up its hair when angry or scared.

A chimpanzee's arms are longer than its legs. Chimps are called knuckle-walkers because they walk on all fours. They walk on two legs for short distances.

Chimpanzees have opposable thumbs and big toes. Their thumbs and toes make it possible for chimps to grip objects and swing from branches.

Life in Africa

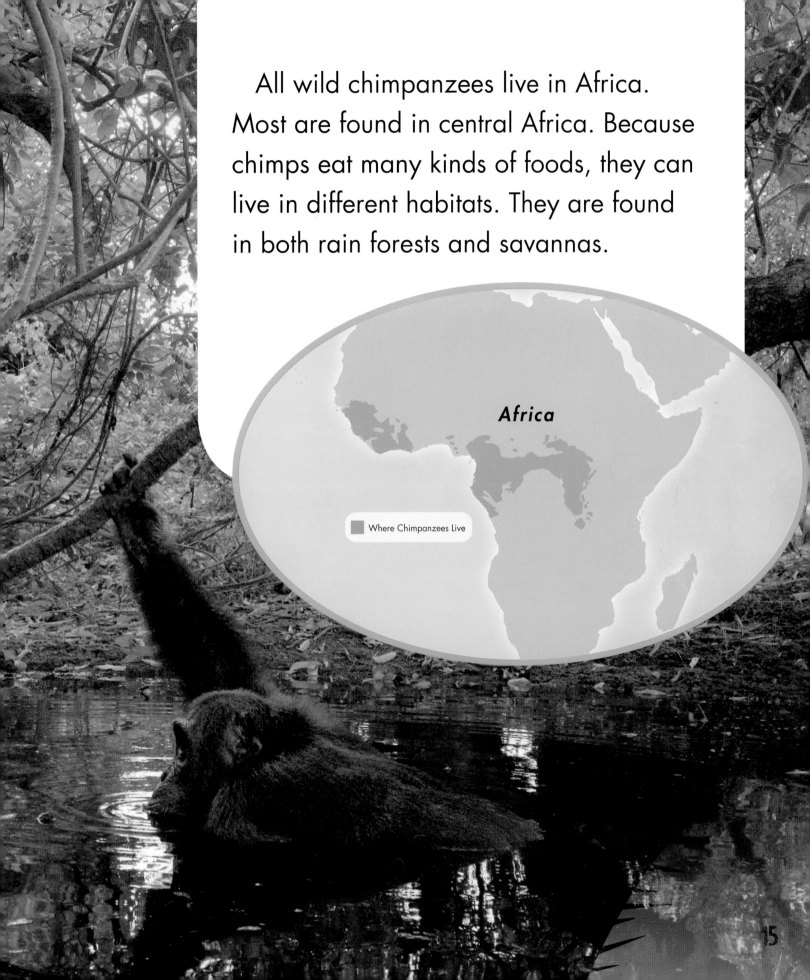

All wild chimpanzees live in Africa. Most are found in central Africa. Because chimps eat many kinds of foods, they can live in different habitats. They are found in both rain forests and savannas.

Africa

Where Chimpanzees Live

Chimpanzees live in groups called communities. Each community has between 15 and 120 chimps. One male leads each community. Chimpanzees eat, sleep, and travel in smaller groups of about six chimps.

Sometimes the entire community
gathers together. The chimpanzees
play and groom one another.
It's like a party for chimps!

Chimpanzees spend most of their days eating and looking for food. They eat fruit, nuts, seeds, leaves, insects, and small animals. They walk the forest floor and climb trees. When one chimp finds food, it lets out a loud call. Other chimps come to enjoy the feast.

Do you use a fork or spoon when you eat? Chimpanzees also use tools at mealtime. They break open nuts with rocks. They scoop water from hollow trees using leaves.

Chimps "fish" for termites and ants by poking sticks into their nests. Then they pull out the sticks and lick off the bugs. They even use leaves for napkins!

At night chimpanzees snooze in trees. They build nests of twigs and branches. Most nests sit at least 15 feet (4.6 meters) above the ground. Chimpanzees make new nests each night.

Each chimp sleeps in its own nest. They rest
their heads on pillows made from soft leaves.

Growing Up Chimpanzee

Female chimpanzees give birth to a single baby after about eight months. Baby chimps are called infants. At birth, infants weigh about 4 pounds (1.8 kg). They have light-colored faces and a small patch of white hair on their rumps.

Female chimpanzees and their young have strong bonds. Infants hitch a ride on their mothers' backs for about two years. Mothers groom their young. They teach them how to crack open nuts and build nests.

Young chimps live with their mothers for six to nine years. But they remain close for life. In the wild chimpanzees can live up to 45 years.

Saving Chimpanzees

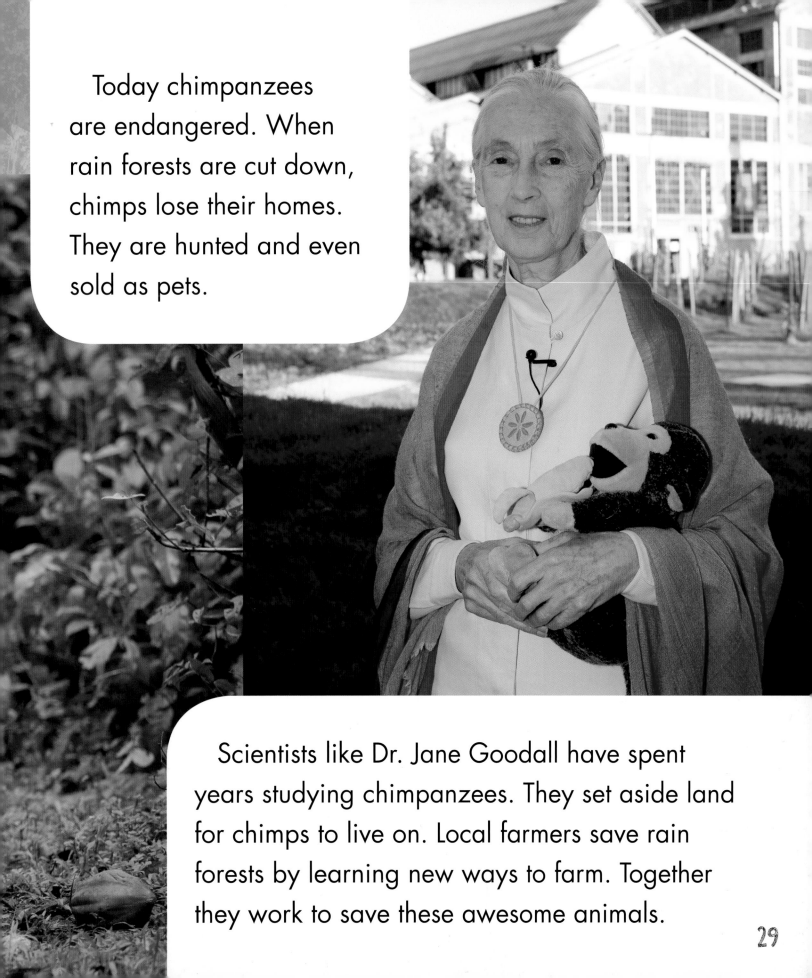

Today chimpanzees are endangered. When rain forests are cut down, chimps lose their homes. They are hunted and even sold as pets.

Scientists like Dr. Jane Goodall have spent years studying chimpanzees. They set aside land for chimps to live on. Local farmers save rain forests by learning new ways to farm. Together they work to save these awesome animals.

Glossary

ape (APE)—a large primate with no tail; gorillas, orangutans, and chimpanzees are kinds of apes

bond (BAHND)—feeling close to someone

communicate (kuh-MYOO-nuh-kate)—to pass along thoughts, feelings, or information

community (kuh-MYOO-nuh-tee)—a population of chimpanzees living together in the same area and depending on each other

endangered (in-DAYN-juhrd)—in danger of dying out

groom (GROOM)—to clean or to make an animal look clean

habitat (HAB-uh-tat)—the natural place and conditions in which a plant or animal lives

opposable (uh-POH-suh-BUHL)—able to be placed against one or more of the other fingers or toes on the same hand or foot

primate (PRYE-mate)—any member of the group of intelligent animals that includes humans, apes, and monkeys

rain forest (RAYN FOR-ist)—a thick forest where a great deal of rain falls

savanna (suh-VAN-uh)—a flat, grassy area of land with some trees

sense (SENSS)—one of the powers a living being uses to learn about its surroundings; sight, hearing, touch, taste, and smell are the five senses

social (SOH-shuhl)—living in groups or packs

Read More

Owen, Ruth. *Chimpanzees. The World's Smartest Animals.* New York: Windmill Books, 2012.

Spilsbury, Louise. *Save the Chimpanzee. Animal SOS!* New York: PowerKids Press, 2014.

Internet Sites

FactHound offers a safe, fun way to find Internet sites related to this book. All of the sites on FactHound have been researched by our staff.

Here's all you do:
Visit *www.facthound.com*
Type in this code: 9781491417591

 Check out projects, games and lots more at **www.capstonekids.com**

Critical Thinking Using the Common Core

1. Look at the pictures on pages 20–21. Describe how the chimpanzees' use of tools is similar to a human's. (Integration of Knowledge and Ideas)

2. On page 22, the text says chimpanzees make their nests at least 15 feet off the ground. Why don't they build their nests on the ground? (Integration of Knowledge and Ideas)

3. How do chimpanzees communicate? Explain how each form of communication might be useful to a chimpanzee community. (Key Ideas and Details)

Index